HAL•LEONARD®

CELLO
PLAY-ALONG

AUDIO
ACCESS
INCLUDED

VOL. 2

STAR WARS: THE FORCE AWAKENS
MUSIC FROM THE MOTION PICTURE SOUNDTRACK

PLAYBACK+
Speed • Pitch • Balance • Loop

To access audio visit:
www.halleonard.com/mylibrary

Enter Code
6008-3102-1868-7132

ISBN 978-1-4950-6003-8

© 2016 & TM Lucasfilm Ltd. All Rights Reserved.

Trischa Loebl, cello

Audio Arrangements by Peter Deneff
Recorded and Produced
at Beat House Music

Utapau Music

DISTRIBUTED BY

7777 W. BLUEMOUND RD. P.O. BOX 13819 MILWAUKEE, WI 53213

Visit Hal Leonard Online at
www.halleonard.com

In Australia Contact:
Hal Leonard Australia Pty. Ltd.
4 Lentara Court
Cheltenham, Victoria, 3192 Australia
Email: ausadmin@halleonard.com.au

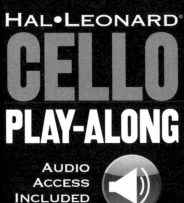

HAL•LEONARD®
CELLO
PLAY-ALONG

AUDIO
ACCESS
INCLUDED

STAR WARS: THE FORCE AWAKENS
MUSIC FROM THE MOTION PICTURE SOUNDTRACK

CONTENTS

Main Title *and* The Attack on the Jakku Village

Music by John Williams

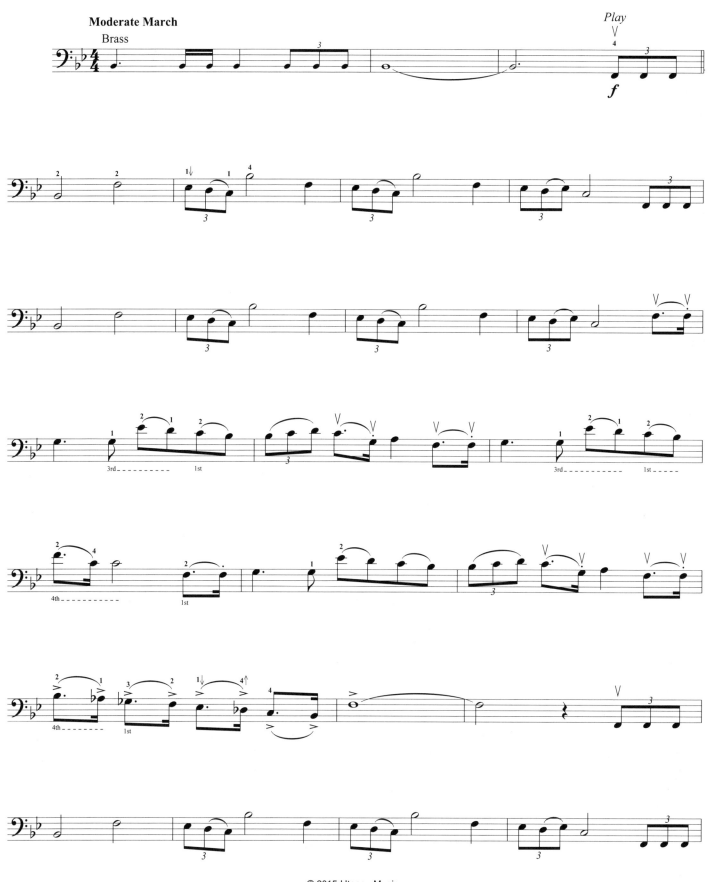

Moderately fast

3rd - - - - - - - - - - - - - -

mp   *pp* > *ppp*

Rey's Theme

Music by John Williams

Finn's Confession

Music by John Williams

Han and Leia

Music by John Williams

March of the Resistance

Music by John Williams

Farewell *and* The Trip

Music by John Williams

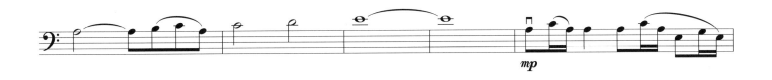

Jedi Steps *and* Finale

Music by John Williams

Torn Apart

Music by John Williams